T0379015

SIAMESE

MARYSA STORM

BLACK
RABBIT
BOOKS

Bolt Jr. is published by Black Rabbit Books
P.O. Box 227, Mankato, Minnesota, 56002.
www.blackrabbitbooks.com
Copyright © 2025 Black Rabbit Books

Alissa Thielges, editor
Rhea Magaro, designer

Names: Storm, Marysa, author.
Title: Siamese / by Marysa Storm.
Description: Mankato, MN: Black Rabbit Books, [2025] | Series: Bolt Jr. Our favorite cats | Includes bibliographical references and index. | Audience: Ages 5–8 | Audience: Grades K–1
Identifiers: LCCN 2024010413 (print) | LCCN 2024010414 (ebook) | ISBN 9781644666807 (library binding) | ISBN 9781644666982 (ebook)
Subjects: LCSH: Siamese cat—Juvenile literature.
Classification: LCC SF449.S5 S765 2025 (print) | LCC SF449.S5 (ebook) | DDC 636.8/25—dc23/eng/20240423
LC record available at https://lccn.loc.gov/2024010413
LC ebook record available at https://lccn.loc.gov/2024010414

Image Credits
Alamy/Petra Wegner, 18; Getty Images/Beachmite Photography, 5; Shutterstock/BearFotos, 10, Bershadsky Yuri, 20–21, Eric Isselee, 8–9, GoodFocused, 13, John Danow, cover, 23, lithian, 17, Liza_Bird, 19, Minerva Studio, 1, Nelli Shuyskaya, 14, Nynke van Holten, 7, Olya Detry, 12, Polina Tomtosova, 3, 24, Serge75, 21, Thanchanok Thammasakjinda, 11, Vasiliy Koval, 4, Voraorn Ratanakorn, 6

Contents

CHAPTER 1

Meet the Siamese

A young girl sits down to read.

Soon, her cat is right by her side.

It is a Siamese cat. It meows loudly.

It **wriggles** onto her lap. It is not

time to read. It is time to cuddle!

wriggle: to twist side to side quickly

COMPARING WEIGHTS

Siamese ◀ ·········· **WEIGHTS**···

11 to 14 pounds

Long Cats

Siamese cats love to be around their owners. They are sweet cats. They have long bodies. Their legs and tails are long too. They are mostly white or cream. Their ears, tails, and faces are darker.

· · · · · · · · · · ▶ **Ragdoll**
10 to 20 pounds
(4.5 to 9 kg)

PARTS OF A
Siamese

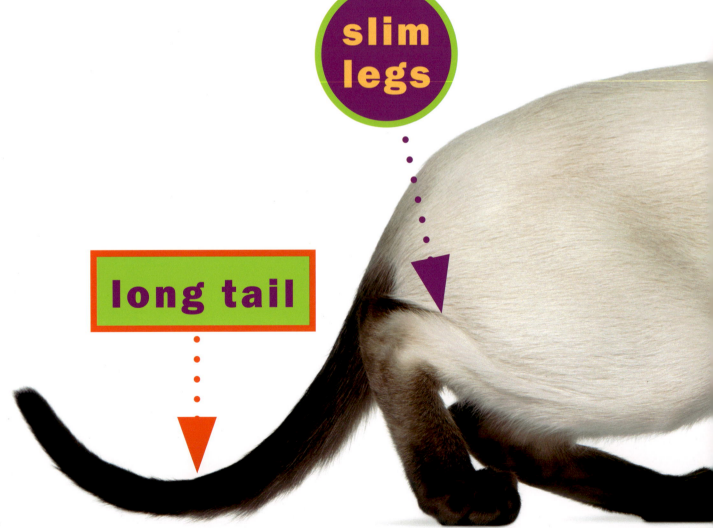

tall ears

slim legs

long tail

blue eyes

long neck

oval paws

9

Personality

Siamese cats love **attention**. They follow their owners around. A Siamese cat cannot be left alone for too long. It will get bored. It might knock things over. It might dig in houseplants.

attention: to notice someone or something

FACT

These cats make a lot of noise.

Smart Cats

These cats are smart. They like a **challenge**. Puzzle games are fun toys. These cats also have a lot of **energy**. It is important to play with them every day.

challenge: to test the ability, skill, or strength of something

energy: the ability to be active

Where They Came From

North America

14

Thailand

15

CHAPTER 3

Siamese Care

Siamese cats have short coats. But they still need weekly brushing. Owners need to make sure these cats don't overeat. They gain weight easily.

FACT
Owners need to brush their cats' teeth too.

Lots of Care

These cats need lots of care. They also need plenty of attention. Siamese cats keep their owners busy. But these cats make great family pets.

Siamese Height
8 to 10 inches
(20–25 centimeters) tall

Bonus Facts

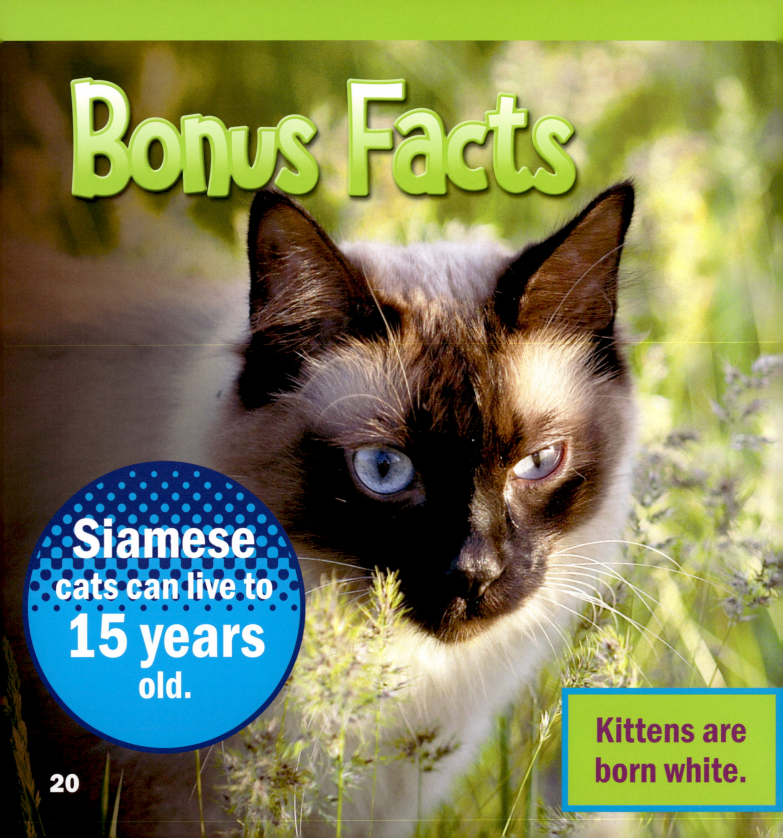

Siamese cats can live to **15 years** old.

Kittens are born white.

They were once kept by **royalty**.

They came to the United States in 1878.

royalty: a member of the ruling family

21

READ MORE/WEBSITES

Andrews, Elizabeth. *Siamese Cats.* Minneapolis: Cody Koala, an imprint of Pop!, 2023.

Burling, Alexis. *Cats.* Minneapolis: Abdo Publishing Company, 2024.

Noelle, Becky. *Siamese.* New York: Lightbox Learning, Inc., 2024.

Siamese
kids.britannica.com/students/article/Siamese/313528

Siamese (Cat) Facts for Kids
kids.kiddle.co/Siamese_(cat)

Siamese Cats
https://cats.com/cat-breeds/siamese

GLOSSARY

attention (uh-TEN-shuhn)— to notice someone or something

challenge (CHAL-inj)— to test the ability, skill, or strength of something

energy (EN-er-jee)— the ability to be active

royalty (ROY-uhl-tee)— a member of the ruling family

wriggle (RIG-uhl)— to twist side to side quickly

INDEX